THE TAOIST VISION

The

Taoist Vision

—

Edited, with an Introduction
and New Translations,
by
WILLIAM MCNAUGHTON

Ann Arbor Paperbacks
THE UNIVERSITY OF MICHIGAN PRESS

Material from *The Classic Anthology* reprinted by permission of the publishers from Ezra Pound, trans., *The Classic Anthology Defined by Confucius*, Cambridge, Mass.: Harvard University Press, Copyright 1954, by the President and Fellows of Harvard College; from Ezra Pound, *The Cantos*, Copyright 1940 by Ezra Pound, reprinted by permission of New Directions Publishing Corporation and of Faber and Faber, Ltd.; "Sennin Poem by Kakuhaku," "Leave-taking Near Shoku," and "Ancient Wisdom, Rather Cosmic," from Ezra Pound, *Personae*, Copyright 1926 by Ezra Pound, reprinted by permission of New Directions Publishing Corporation and from *Collected Shorter Poems of Ezra Pound*, reprinted by permission of Faber and Faber, Ltd.; "Answering Vice-Prefect Chang," from C. H. Kwock and Vincent McHugh, *Why I Live on the Mountain*, © Copyright 1958 by C. H. Kwock and Vincent McHugh, reprinted by permission of Vincent McHugh; "The Magic Pillow," from Wang Chi-chen, *Traditional Chinese Tales*, Copyright 1967 by Chi-chen Wang, reprinted by permission of Chi-chen Wang; "Classic Scene" and "Fine Work with Pitch and Copper," from William Carlos Williams, *The Collected Earlier Poems*, Copyright 1938 by William Carlos Williams, reprinted by permission of New Directions Publishing Corporation, and of Macgibbon & Kee Ltd., publishers for the British Commonwealth except Canada; "Pity this busy monster manunkind," from E. E. Cummings, *Poems 1923–1954*, Copyright 1944 by E. E. Cummings, reprinted by permission of Harcourt Brace Jovanovich, Inc.; "n" and "seeker of truth," from E. E. Cummings, *73 Poems*, © 1961, 1963 by Marion Morehouse Cummings, reprinted by permission of Harcourt Brace Jovanovich, Inc.; in the British Commonwealth except Canada, Cummings' poems from *Complete Poems 1936–1962*, reprinted by permission of Macgibbon & Kee, Ltd., translations and poem by Lenore Mayhew, © 1971 by Lenore Mayhew, reprinted by permission of Lenore Mayhew.

1

INTRODUCTION

Of "the religions of China," one—Buddhism—came in from India, and two—Confucianism and Taoism—grew up in China herself. That kind of Buddhism which is "most Chinese"—namely, Zen Buddhism—is just Buddhism transformed by Taoism. In this book, I propose to introduce the reader to one of the two native Chinese religions—Taoism.

Taoism is "the philosophy of the Tao." What the Tao is, we will get to later. The Chinese themselves usually call Taoism "Lao-Chuang philosophy," because the two most important Taoist philosophers were Lao Tzu (sixth century B.C.) and Chuang Tzu (fourth century B.C.). Taoism rests on two books: Lao Tzu's *Tao Te Ching* and Chuang Tzu's *Chuang Tzu's Book*.

In *The Taoist Vision,* the reader will find: 1) the crucial passage, from the *Tao Te Ching* or from *Chuang Tzu's Book,* in which each basic Taoist idea is introduced; 2) an anthology of Chinese literature, affirming Taoist values; 3) a selection of Japanese poems with Taoist subjects; 4) some modern poetry, both Oriental and Western, in which the Taoist vision reappears; 5) reproductions of three great Taoist paintings. Perhaps the combination of abstract philosophical discussion and concrete verbal and visual presentation will enable the reader to see the Taoist vision, and to understand what he is seeing. Maybe, for a moment at least, these Taoist classics will affirm Yeats' lines:

> This preposterous pragmatical pig of a world
> Would vanish on the instant if the mind but change
> its theme.

Of all the Eastern ideas recently to receive attention in the West, I think none has been more useful than those belonging to Taoism. One man has used Taoist ideas to argue that we should put all the metals back in the ground. Two or three others have seen Taoism as the advent, or adjunct, of a new religion. The favorite poet of America's young has used the Tao[1] against locomotives. Early Christian missionaries thought Tao had to do with *logos*. It gets harder and harder to understand our own literature if we do not know something about Taoism.

In the first half of *The Taoist Vision,* the reader can read what Lao Tzu and Chuang Tzu themselves had to say about the basic concepts. The basic Taoist concepts—concepts is such a pretentious word for a book about Taoism, call them "the usual subjects of conversation among Taoists"—are Tao, darkness, water, the 'uncarved block,' emptiness, energy, anti-action, transformation, and self-like-ness (chaps. 3–

11, 17–24). The reader also can read, in Lao Tzu's own words, about the relation of Taoist values to the other basic Chinese values—Confucian values—like rites, humanity, equity, and learning (chaps. 12–15).

In the second half of *The Taoist Vision,* the reader will read other Chinese—some of them earlier even than Lao Tzu—who had the Taoist vision and who "corrected themselves by peace and quiet." And he will read poets and prose-writers, Chinese and Japanese, and even modern Westerners like Cummings and Williams, who have seen the world in a Taoist eye.

I have retranslated all material from the two philosophical classics, *Tao Te Ching* and *Chuang Tzu's Book.* Of material translated from authors other than Lao Tzu and Chuang Tzu, I have done the translation unless another translator is identified.

Book One

A PRIMER ON TAOISM

Part One
The Tao (Tao)

2

THE OLD GUY

Lao Tzu was born about 570 B.C., if you follow the tradition. We do not know when he died. They say he met Confucius between 518 and 511 B.C. The Chinese words "Lao Tzu" are not really a name, but mean "the Old Guy."

LAO TZU: A BIOGRAPHY
From Ssu-ma Ch'ien's *Historical Records*[2]

Lao Tzu was a native of Ch'u-jen Village, Li County, K'u State, Ch'u Province. His surname was Li ("Plum"), his name was Erh ("Ears"), his formal name was Po-yang, and his spiritual name is Tan.

Lao Tzu worked as keeper of the Royal Archives for the Eastern Chou Dynasty rulers. When Confucius visited the Chou court, he went to Lao Tzu to

7

ask about the rules concerning official ritual. While he was there, Lao Tzu said to him, "This 'superior man' that you are talking about, his body and bones already have rotted away. All that's left of him is those three or four sentences. When a superior man lives in a congenial age, he goes to court in a carriage. When a superior man lives in an uncongenial age, he walks away with both hands on his hat. From what I hear, when a true businessman has a good thing, he tucks it away and keeps it quiet; and when a superior man truly has the virtue, to look at his face you'd think he was simple-minded. Get rid of all this dignity and pretense, get rid of all this pose and aspiration. None of it does you any good. I thought I'd tell you about these things, because this is the way it is."

Afterward, when Confucius was with his students again, he said to them: "Birds, I understand how they fly. Fish, I understand how they swim. Animals, I understand how they run. What runs, you can take with a snare. What swims, you can take with a line. What flies, you can take with a shaft. But as for dragons, I do not understand how they ride the winds and clouds and sail over the sky. I saw Lao Tzu today. He is a dragon, all right."

Lao Tzu developed and practiced the Tao and its Energy, but this was a hermetic art he practiced by himself. It was not a "How To . . ." that he publicized or sold. He lived at the Chou Court for a long time. When he saw the art of government fade out there and die, he finally left the place. When Lao Tzu came to the border, a passport officer named Hsi said to him, "You're going to leave here and hide yourself away: but not until you've written me a book." So Lao Tzu sat down and wrote the book for him. The book has a first part and a second part, and it's all about the Tao and the Te. There is something over five thousand words in it. He wrote it and left the Province, and nobody knows where he went.

They say, "Lao Lai-tzu also was from Ch'u Province, and he wrote a book in fifteen chapters, and the book is full of Taoists and their usual subjects of conversation, and he was a contemporary of Confucius." If we follow them, Lao Tzu lived to be over a hundred and sixty years old.

They say, "Lao Tzu lived more than two hundred years, because he practiced the Tao, that's how he was able to live so long." And they say Grand Historian Tan who went to see the 'Gift-giving Duke' of Ch'in was Lao Tzu. And some say that's a lot of nonsense. The truth is, we moderns don't know whether Grand Historian Tan was Lao Tzu or not.

We might say, "Lao Tzu was a *hermetic* 'superior man.' " Today's men that study Lao Tzu scorn Confucian scholarship, and today's Confucian scholars scorn Lao Tzu. Their doctrines are not the same, they cannot work together. How could it be otherwise? Lao Erh changed himself by anti-action, and he corrected himself by peace and quiet.

3

THE DEFINITION OF 'TAO'

Knowers don't speak. Speakers don't know.

Know you don't know: that's superior. Look, if you have flaws and say they're flaws, that's how you lack flaws. The sage lacks flaws. He takes his flaws to be flaws, and that's how he lacks flaws.

DEFINITION

The tao you can tao is not the Tao. The name you can name is not the Name.

4

THE DARKNESS OF THE TAO (*Hsuan*)

What isn't, we call the beginning of Heaven and
Earth. What is, we call the Mother of the ten thousand things. Therefore, the eternal "what isn't," we
want to look at its subtlety; the eternal "what is," we
want to look at its substance.

"What is," "what isn't," came out together but
got different names: together we call them *hsuan*—
dark. This is darkness again darkened—the gate of all
subtlety.

You may look at it and not see it: we call it "the
uncommon." You may listen to it but not hear it: we
call it "the extra-ordinary." You may touch it but not
feel it: we call it "the subtle." These three things cannot be investigated in detail, so we lump them together to form one. . . . It runs on and on and cannot
be named. It returns again to the immaterial. We call
it the form that never forms, the image that never
materializes.

When the tao becomes a thing, it evades and
eludes; eludes, evades: within it there's an image;
evades, eludes; within it there's a thing.

There is a thing, undefined and perfect, which was produced before Heaven and Earth. Vast! Waste! It alone stands and does not flow. Entering everywhere, it does not impinge. We may take it as Mother of everything under Heaven. I don't know what it's named. I call it "tao." I'm forced to name it "the great." "Great," that's to extend. "Extend," that's to recede. "Recede," that's to return.

Man's rule is earth. Earth's rule is Heaven. Heaven's rule is Tao. Tao's rule is "Selflike."

5

WATER

The highest good is like water. Water well-benefits the ten thousand things and does not strain. It rests in places that most people despise, and so it approaches the tao.

6

THE UNCARVED BLOCK

Though the uncarved block is pretty small, nothing under Heaven can govern it. When the first principle gets a name, names there will be but good. You will know, then, that this is where to stop.

7

THE EMPTINESS OF THE TAO (*Hsu*)

The thirty spokes join on the one hub, and their usefulness for the carriage is just where they aren't. You take a clay lump to make the dish, and the clay's usefulness is just where it isn't. You cut material into doors and windows to make a room, and its usefulness as a room is just where it isn't. So you take what of it there is to use what of it there isn't.

The space between Heaven and Earth, well, is like a bellows: it's empty and inexhaustible, it moves and continues to emerge . . . Use it. It will not wear out.

Heaven extends. Earth endures.

Use the Tao's emptiness; it will never be filled.

8

SCHOLAR RECLINING

Ma Lin, Sung Dynasty
SCHOLAR RECLINING AND WATCHING RISING CLOUDS
Courtesy The Cleveland Museum of Art, John L. Severance Fund

Part Two
Energy (Te)

9

THE "DARKER ENERGY"

To bear, to rear—don't possess what you produce, don't covet what you create, don't rush what you raise. This we call the "darker energy."

10

ANTI-ACTION[3]

The tao removes to move. The tao weakens to use.
The ten thousand things under Heaven come from
what there is. What there is comes from what there
isn't.

What you want to shrink, you first must stretch.
What you want to enervate, you first must energize.—
What you want to lay low, you first must set up; what
you want to grab, you first must give.

This I would call a subtle light: the tender and
weak overcomes the hard and strong.

Tao never seeks, and never lacks, effect.

"Breaks" becomes "perfects," "bends" becomes
"straightens," "empties" becomes "fills," "spoils" becomes "renews," "cuts down" becomes "adds on,"
"augments" becomes "confuses."

The tree you barely can reach around grows from
the thinnest shoot. The tower that's ten stories tall
rises from a layer of dirt. The journey that's a thousand *li* begins under your very foot.

Well to act the soldier, one will not be martial.
Well to act the belligerent, one will not be hostile.

Well to conquer a foe, one will not engage with him. Well to use another, you will become his subordinate. This is called the effect of failing to strive. This is called the advantage of using others.

Effectively to learn, is daily to add on. Effectively to tao, is daily to cut down. Cut it down and again cut down, and never fail to affect.

Therefore, the sage rests in the work of anti-action, and spreads the doctrine of not lecturing.

Gain the world? Always accept the anti-event. To reach to the event itself is to fail to gain the world.[4]

That on which the sea and the Yang-tze depend to rule the hundred streams is, they are well lower than they, so that they become the hundred streams' rulers.

Of all things under Heaven, none is more tender and weak than water; but to attack the firm and the strong, nothing can surpass it. Now what it changes is its what it's not. That weak overcomes strong, that tender overcomes firm, no one under Heaven but knows it, and yet no one can practice it.

Acting, anti-act; working, anti-work; tasting, anti-taste. Magnify the minima, multiply the dividua. Respond to grief with joy. Prepare for the difficult in the easy. Deal with the big in the small. Difficult undertakings must be done in the easy, and great undertakings must be done in the small. Therefore the sage never strives for the great, and thereby he is able to achieve this "great."

Move toward the extreme that is empty. Hold to the reality that is silent. The ten thousand things interact, and so I watch for the rebound.

11

THE "HIGHER ENERGY"

The higher energy is not energetic, that's why it has energy. The lower energy is not inert, that's why it lacks energy. The higher energy never seeks, and never lacks, effect. The lower energy seeks it and always lacks it.

Part Three
The Social Order

12
MANNERS AND MODE OF CONDUCT (*L I*)[5]

The higher good nature works by never taking action. The higher sense of proportion works, yes, by taking action. The higher manners and mode of conduct *(li)*, taking action and getting no result, will dust up if not polish off.

Therefore, lose the tao, and then your energy; lose your energy, and then your good nature; lose your good nature, and then your sense of proportion; lose your sense of proportion, and then your manners and mode of conduct.[6] Manners and mode of conduct, then, is the attenuation of loyalty and of creditability, and is the thin edge of chaos.

13

"HUMANITY" (JEN) AND "EQUITY" (I)

When the great tao is gone, "humanity" and "equity" appear.[7] When "intellect" and "education" emerge, the great fakes will appear. When the six relations[8] do not harmonize, "filiality" and "affection" will appear. When the state breaks up or breaks down, the "statesmen" and "patriots" will appear.

Heaven is not "humane," and Earth is not "humane." They take the ten thousand things as dogs of straw. The sage is not "humane." He takes the hundred clans as dogs of straw.

14

EDUCATION (*CHIH*)

Everybody knows beauty as "beauty." That's pretty ugly. Everybody knows good as "good." That's pretty bad.

The five colors make a man's eye blind. The five tones make a man's ear deaf. The five flavors make a man's mouth insensitive.

True words are not beautiful, beautiful words are not true. Good men don't argue, arguers aren't good. Knowers aren't learned, the learned don't know.

The sage learns to unlearn his learning.

Music and the smell of good cooking will make the passing traveler stop. But the taste the Tao gives is insipid and without savor.

Of insufficiencies, none is greater than not to know what's enough. Of disasters, none is greater than the urge to acquire. So the only "enough" that's enough is to know what's enough.

Sever study, never worry.

As for "unh . . .," to what extent may we dissociate it from "yeah!"? As for "good," how shall we dissociate it from "evil"?

For whoever believes insufficiently in others, there will be those that do not believe in him.

When a first-rate scholar hears of the tao, he starts to practice it. When a second-rate scholar hears of the tao, he either concentrates on it or forgets about it. When a third-rate scholar hears of the tao, he has a big laugh about it. If he didn't, it wouldn't be worthy to call the tao.

15

GOVERNMENT

The ruler who has in him the tao doesn't try to push everybody around with force of arms. A thing like that is apt to bounce.

Where an army has camped, thorns and brambles spring up. After great armies, there must be years of famine and disease.

There are many "don'ts" and taboos in the world, yet the people suffer all kinds of things. The people have many sophisticated weapons, and the country is the more harassed. People are more erudite, more educated, and unforeseen things the more often occur. The more the laws and codes are displayed, the more thieves and crooks there are.

"1) Break up 'wisdom' and kick out education,' the people will profit a hundredfold. 2) Break up 'humanity,' and kick out "righteousness," the people once more will be filial and affectionate. 3) Break up 'talent' and kick out 'capability,' thieves and crooks will disappear." It may be assumed that the complementation of these three is inadequate. So there must be something which they subserve: see the unrefined and seize the unprocessed, minimize the self and diminish its desires.

Don't exalt talent, and the people won't contend. Don't prize goods that are hard to acquire, and the people will not become thieves. Don't show off desirables, and the people's minds will not grow wild.

What of it? The sage will govern like this: empty their minds, fill their bellies, weaken their ambitions, strengthen their bones. It will make the people never to know and never to yearn, and it will keep the so-called intelligentsia timid to act.

What is most high? That of which those below know only that it exists.

What is next most high? That which they affect and talk up.

What is next lower to this? That which they fear.

What is lower still? That which they ridicule.

Part Four
Transformation

———

16

"MR. COOL"

Chuang-tzu lived from 365 to 290 B.C. more or less. His more personal name is Chuang Chou, and Chuang-tzu means "Mr. Chuang" or "the Chuang" (the way the English used to refer to their nemesis as "the Douglas"). His name Chuang, as a word in Chinese, appropriately enough means "Serene" or "Calm." He came from the state of Sung, in which descendants of the old Shang-Yin Dynasty still lived as princes. His home was well within the field of orthodox and traditional Chinese culture. He held for a time a post as minor clerk in his native district. We don't know much else about him. His political career is described in the following story:

Chuang-tzu was fishing one time in the P'u River. Two ministers came up. They said they were ministers from the King of Ch'u. The King of Ch'u wanted Chuang-tzu to come and run his kingdom for him.

Chuang-tzu sat there and held his fishing pole. He didn't even turn around. And he said to the ministers, "Doesn't your king have a sacred tortoise that's been dead for three thousand years, and doesn't the king keep his tortoise wrapped up and in a box and stored in his ancestral temple"?

"Yes, that's no lie," said the ministers.

And Chuang-tzu said, "This tortoise, is he better off dead and with his bones venerated, or is he better off alive with his tail dragging in the mud"?

And the ministers said, "Better off alive, we suppose, with his tail dragging in the mud."

"Go away," said Chuang-tzu, "and let me drag my tail in the mud."

17

THE BUTTERFLY DREAM

One time, Chuang-tzu dreamed he was a butterfly, flitting around, enjoying what butterflies enjoy. The butterfly did not know that it was Chuang-tzu. Then Chuang-tzu started, and woke up, and he was Chuang-tzu again. And he began to wonder, whether he was Chuang-tzu who had dreamed he was a butterfly, or was a butterfly dreaming that he was Chuang-tzu.

18

THREE IN THE MORNING

There was a man who kept monkeys. He told the monkeys, one time, that their acorns would be rationed: each monkey would get three acorns in the morning, and four acorns in the evening. The monkeys were infuriated. And so the keeper said, "Look, I am not an unreasonable man. We will change this. Each of you may have four acorns in the morning, and three acorns in the evening." And with this, the monkeys all were pleased.[9]

19

FIVE PERSIMMONS

Mu Ch'i (1180–1250)
FIVE PERSIMMONS
Daitokuji, Kyoto

31

Part Five

"The Tao's Rule"

20

"SELF-LIKE-NESS"

The Tao does not begin, the Tao does not end. Things come into being and vanish: they hold no permanence. Things are sometimes empty, things are sometimes full: they hold no constant form. You cannot detain the years, or cause time to hesitate. Increase and decrease go on and on, and whatever ends, has begun. So we talk about a "great norm" and say that some Principle runs through everything.

So some people say the natural holds on within, and the artificial holds on without, and *te* inheres in the natural. Know how nature moves and how man moves, take nature as your basis and *te* as your "still point," and you may without anxiety proceed or recede, shrink or expand: for things return always to essences and to ultimates.

33

So some people say, don't wipe out the natural with the artificial. Don't wipe out destiny with effort. Don't spoil your delight for fame's sake. Do it like this, and you may return to origins and to innocence.

21

Chuang-tzu and Hui-tzu were walking around one day. They walked over the Bridge on the River Hao. "Look," said Chuang-tzu. "Those little fish leap and dance around wherever they want. That's the delight the fish have."

And Hui-tzu said, "Chuang-tzu, you are not a fish. How do you know what delight the fish have?"

Chuang-tzu said, "Hui-tzu, you are not I. How do you know I don't know what delight the fish have?"

22

PRINCE YUAN OF SUNG'S PORTRAIT

Prince Yuan of Sung wished to have his portrait painted. All the official painters were notified. They came to the Prince and bowed. At the Prince's command, they stood attentive and expectant. They licked their brushes, mixed their ink, and waited. At about that moment, which was rather late for it, a certain painter sauntered in. He refused to hurry. The Prince commanded this last painter to bow, which he did. But he would not stand attentive and expectant. Thereupon, the Prince ordered that he be given a place to stay. The Prince sent an intelligence agent to discover what the person did in his rooms. When the agent returned, he reported that the painter "took off his clothes and squatted down barebacked."

"He will do," said the Prince. "He is a true painter."

23

They called the Emperor of the South Sea "Short." They called the Emperor of the North Sea "Swift." They called the Emperor of the Middle Regions "Strungloose." Short and Swift sometimes went together to see Strungloose. Strungloose always gave them a great time.

Short and Swift decided they should do Strungloose a favor, his hospitality was so good. They had noticed that all men have seven openings so that they can see, hear, eat and breathe. "Strungloose," they said to each other, "doesn't have these openings. Let us bore him some."

So Short and Swift began to bore holes in Strungloose, one a day. On the seventh day, Strungloose died.[10]

24

MONK SEWING

MONK, SEWING

Courtesy The Abbot of Ryoanji Temple, Kyoto, Japan

Book Two

25

THE TAO IN LITERATURE

Classified according to subject, Chinese poetry has about a dozen favorite kinds of poem: homesick, anti-war, separation, history and myth, farm and garden, mountains and rivers, eros, "seraglio," "sennin," "embrace the ancient," "sunging" (seeing off a friend), and "the moment." Of this dozen, three kinds of poem are distinctly and indubitably 'Taoist': "farm and garden" poems, "sennin" poems, and poems about "the moment."

In the farm and garden poem, the Chinese poet tells us that he no longer intends to "sacrifice for fame's sake" but intends to enjoy the simple pleasures of living at home, watching children grow, and taking care of his garden. T'ao Ch'ien, the archetypical Chinese "farm and garden poet," writes:

> Now that they reclaim
> > the Southern moors
> I, holding to my stupidity,
> > reclaim a farm and garden for myself

(see Chapter 27).

The "sennin" is a man who has given up usual human pursuits—wealth, or fame, or power—and goes to live an isolated life in the mountains. The Chinese character for the word "sennin" is a "man" beside a "mountain." All sorts of myths sprung up about sennin, sennin were said to have discovered the elixir of life, to have supernatural powers, etc. The only thing that can be said about them for sure is that they did not cultivate S/society, with a capital "S" or a small "s".

The poem about "the moment," I believe, operates within the principle rediscovered by modern artists, "so to concentrate the mind on a single rhythm, defined plane, object, scene, or thing, that it becomes more conscious of all things, scenes, objects, defined planes, or rhythms." The principle, and "the moment" as a subject for poetry, fit into classical Taoism at the point where Lao Tzu says,

> Everybody knows beauty as 'Beauty.' That's pretty ugly. Everybody knows good as 'Good.' That's pretty bad.
> The five colors make a man's eye blind. The five tones make a man's ear deaf. The five flavors make a man's mouth insensitive.

4 0

The poem about "the moment" says, "There is no Beauty, but only this particular thing, whether it is a cardinal, or a powerhouse, or a frog and his pond:"

> An ancient pool
> and a leaping frog—
> the water's sound!

Japanese Zen, like its philosophical parent Chinese Ch'an, owes much of its outlook to Taoism. The Japanese poets, and especially the haiku-poets, wrote many, many poems—like the famous Basho haiku just quoted—in which "the moment" is presented, and the Taoist value is realized. Basho himself said, "A commonplace occurrence, described as it is, is precious; it is wrong to resort to tricks in composing *haiku*. Looking at nature as it is, portraying nature as it is— this should be the haiku-poet's attitude." The tricky phrase in this remark is, "as it is." If the poet merely writes up a commonplace experience as he has been taught to see it, if in it he only sees "Beauty," and the "five colors," and hears in it only "the five sounds," then he has not done the thing.

Or take Monet, on the significance of the Japanese print show in Paris and its result, Impressionism: *Ce que nous avons surtout apprecié, c'est un façon hardi de couper le sujet.* They learned how effectively to tao it.

26

THE POETRY CLASSIC

According to the official histories, Confucius returned from Wei to Lu in 484 B.C. and brought with him songs gathered on his travels. He is supposed to have picked the three hundred best of some three thousand songs he knew and to have made of them an anthology, called by men of later generations *The Poetry Classic*. Many scholars see in *The Poetry Classic* a poetic exposition of Confucian doctrine, and it also has been called *The Confucian Anthology*. But so broad is the scope, that we also can find songs that express Taoist points of view. Since Chinese poetry begins with *The Poetry Classic,* it seems like a good idea to begin our reading of Taoist literature with some poems from it. The poems given all are supposed to have been composed between 781 and 696 B.C. If nothing else, that proves that Lao Tzu was not the first Taoist.

LET THE GREAT CART ALONE

Let the Great Cart alone,
'ware dust.
Think not on sorrows
lest thy heart rust.

Push no great cart
lest dust enflame thine eye,
brood not on sorrows
lest joy pass by.

Push not the great wheel-spoke
in moil and sweat
lest thou make thy troubles
heavier yet.

(bet. 781 and 770 B.C.)

(translated by Ezra Pound)

43

'NEATH THICK WILLOW

'Neath the thick willow, 'tis good to lie.
Let the Imperial foot pass by
If he gi' me a low job, it would lift me too high.

Better stay 'neath the willow bough
than crush a toe beneath the Imperial car,
if he gave me a lift, it would take me too far.

A bird can circle high over cloud,
a man's mind will lift above the crowd
reaching employ on high above us all
to dwell in deeper misery when he fall.

(bet. 781 and 770 B.C.)

(translated by Ezra Pound)

HUT IN THE VALE

Made his hut in the vale, a tall man stretched out
sleeps, wakes and says: no room for doubt.

Lean-to on torrent's brink, laughter in idleness,
sleeps, wakes and sings: I will move less.

In a hut on a butte, himself his pivot, sleeps,
wakes, sleeps again,
swearing he will not communicate
with other men.

(bet. 770 and 719 B.C.)

(translated by Ezra Pound)

OLE BRER RABBIT WATCHIN' HIS FEET

Ole Brer Rabbit watchin' his feet,
Rabbit net's got the pheasant beat.
I began life with too much elan,
Troubles come to a bustiling man.
                  "Down Oh, and give me a bed!"

Ole Brer Rabbit watchin' his feet,
Pheasant's caught in the rabbit trap.
I began life with a flip and a flap
Then I met trouble?
                      Aye, my son.
           Wish I could sleep till life was done.

Ole Brer Rabbit watchin' his feet,
Rabbit net's got the pheasant beat.
A youngster was always rushin' round,
Troubles crush me to the ground.
          Wish I could sleep and not hear a sound.

                  (bet. 719 and 696 B.C.)

(translated by Ezra Pound)[11]

4 6

27

HAN LING was governed by eunuchs
    wars, murders, and crime news
HAN sank and there were three kingdoms
    and booze in the bamboo grove
where they sang: emptiness is the
    beginning of all things.

—Canto L I V

POEM OF MY HEART

Juan Chi (210–263)

Twelve o'clock.
    Unable to sleep,
I get up and sit,
    I play and sing to the ch'in.
The fragile cloths
    mirror a brilliant moon;
Metallic wind
    agitates my sleeve.
One single crane
    cries past the farthest fields;
Another bird
    sings in the northward grove.
Go back, go forth.
    What shall any of us find?
Sorrowful thoughts.
    Solitude. Shaken nerve.

POEM OF MY HEART

Juan Chi

Cranes, each
    following other, fly
Fly, fly
    going to the wilderness' end.
Double feathers
    reach to the long wind.
Instantly
    they travel a thousand li.
Mornings, they eat
    fruit of the white coral-tree;
Evenings, they stop
    at Cinnabar Mountain's edge.
They lift their bodies
    into the blue clouds.
With net and snare,
    who can bring them in?
How should one,
    with a small-town guy,
Shake hands
    or together swear an oath?

SENNIN POEM

The red and green kingfishers
    flash between the orchids and the clover,
One bird casts its gleam on another.

Green vines hang through the high forest,
They weave a whole roof to the mountain,
The lone man sits with shut speech,
He purrs and pats the clear strings.
He throws his heart up through the sky,
He bites through the flower-pistil
    and brings up a fine fountain.
The red-pine-tree god looks at him and wonders.

He rides through the purple smoke to visit the sennin,
He takes "Floating Hill" by the sleeve,
He claps his hand on the back of the
    great water sennin.

But you, you dam'd crowd of gnats,
Can you even tell the age of a turtle?

(translated by Ezra Pound)

5 0

''TZU YEH'' SONG

Let others find themselves alike,
My will is obstinately I.
My winter blinds are wide to winds
And long, in cold,
                  my curtains fly.

(translated by Lenore Mayhew)

GOING HOME

T'ao Ch'ien (365–427)

When I was small
    I never was like-minded with the others
But had from birth
    a temperament attaching to the hills
And yet by chance
    I fell into the dust net of this world
Where in an instant
    passed some thirty years.

A trapped bird
    will hanker after his old woods
A pooled fish
    will think of his old deeps.
Now that they reclaim
    the southern moors
I, holding to my stupidity,
    reclaim a farm and garden for myself.

With private house
    encircled by its land

Of grass without
 within some nine large rooms in all,
Elm and willow
 shade the eaves in back
And peach and plum
 are planted in straight rows
  before the hall.

Distant villages
 are indistinct
Their thin light smoke
 ten li away.
Dogs bark
 down the long alleys
Chickens cackle
 atop the mulberries
But the dust of my walled courtyard
 is never scattered.

In my empty rooms are time and space.
I was a bird
 confined within a wicker cage
But now I may return
 to be myself
Unfretted and unfettered
 in this self-like place.

(translated by Lenore Mayhew)

53

28

MR. FIVE WILLOWS

THE BIOGRAPHY OF
MR. FIVE WILLOWS

by T'ao Ch'ien

I don't know what place he is a native of. I don't know what his family name is, or his given name, or his "studio name," or his "society name," or his pen name. He has five willow-trees planted beside his house, and we call him "Mr. Five Willows."

He often leaves the bar down across his door, and some people find him taciturn. He does not get very excited about glory or money. They say that he likes to read, but I am afraid *explication de texte* bores him. Wherever there is a felicitous juxtaposition of ideas, he can get so excited about it that he forgets to eat.

Mr. Five Willows likes a glass of wine now and then, but because he does not have a lot of money, he usually has to go without it. His relatives and old friends know this thirst of his, and they sometimes lay in wine and ask him by. When he comes to drink he doesn't stand on ceremony, and he usually does not stop until he is quite drunk. When he is quite drunk, if he feels like staying, he stays; if he feels like going home, he goes home. He may not tell you about it beforehand.

The four walls of his house are falling in, and they let through the wind and the sun. He goes around in a robe of fur that is patched and sewn. His cup and bowl often are empty, but you would think he was at a great banquet.

He often writes on this or that to amuse himself, and he tries clearly to say how he feels about things. He forgets about "the profit and the loss," and I suppose he will go on like this the rest of his life.

We might say, "Chin Lu has said, 'Don't be sad about poverty. Don't be anxious about wealth.' " I think he was talking about the sort of man Mr. Five Willows is. Holding the wine-cup to his lips, writing essays and composing poems, doing what he feels like for his own delight—isn't this "to be a citizen of 'the Serene Emperor,' " isn't this "to be a subject of 'the Bean-flower Emperor'?"

29

PEACH BLOSSOM SPRING

by T'ao Ch'ien

"During the Chin Dynasty's T'ai Yuan period, a certain fisherman lived in Wu-ling. One day, following a stream along its course, this fisherman lost track of distance and time. Suddenly, he found himself at an area where blossoming peach trees lined the banks for hundreds of yards. There were no trees of any other kind, but there were fragant flowers to delight the eye, and peach blossoms drifted everywhere in the air.

"The fisherman was amazed. He decided to push on to see where the peach trees would end. They ended at a spring, and beyond the spring was a hill. The fisherman saw a small opening in the hillside, and he thought he could see a tiniest light within the opening. He climbed from his boat and went into the hillside opening. He had to creep and crawl the first distance, but after a while the passage gave into open air again. He saw the land stretch out level before him. He looked over an area of fine buildings, set among fertile fields and pleasant ponds. There were mulberry trees and willows. The fisherman noticed that paths led here and there. One farm's fowls and dogs could be heard at the next farm. People came and went, or worked in the fields. The men and women were dressed in no extraordinary clothes, and the tufted children and white-haired old folk laughed and played.

"Eventually, a person—then two, then three—noticed the fisherman. They showed some surprise and asked him, Where did he come from? He told them his story.

"He was then invited to people's homes. They served him wine, and killed chickens as for a feast. The news quickly spread through the village, and many people came to see him and to ask him questions. They also told him that their own ancestors, during the Ch'in epoch, had fled from civil disorder and political strife: they had traveled to this hidden place with their neighbors and wives. They knew nothing of what had happened in the Empire since the Ch'in epoch. They had never even heard of the Han Dynasty, nor of the Wei Dynasty nor of the Chin Dynasty which came after the Han. The fisherman satisfied their curosity about the outside world, and they exclaimed with wonder at his tales. He was invited to home after home, and they served him fine food and wine in every one.

"So the fisherman stayed with this people for some time. Finally, however, he took his leave. 'Do not you,' said they, 'speak of us to the world outside.'

"But as the fisherman traveled his homeward way, he took care to mark it league by league. When he had returned to his home country, he went at once to the county magistrate and told him his tale. The magistrate sent a contingent to follow the fisherman to this wonderful community. He hunted for the route he had marked but grew confused and could not find the way. Later on, an erudite and pure-hearted hermit, Liu Tzu-chi, heard of the fisherman's experience. Liu became excited and set out to rediscover the community. But he did not succeed and finally fell ill and died. Since then, no one has 'sought the ford.' "

30

T'ANG POETRY

—Il Signor Stapps aveva in mente una mis-
cellanea di poeti di tutto il mondo, dai
T'ang fino a Rilke, alla dinamite sempre
imperturbabile, avvolto da una nube di
cattiva letteratura.

(EUGENIO MONTALE)

POEM

Wang Wei (699–759)

Under the black
bamboo, he sits
alone

Strikes the lute—
breaks chords
and sings.

And no one
sees this shadowed
place

or rising
moonlight light
his face.

(translated by Lenore Mayhew and
William McNaughton)

ANSWERING VICE-PREFECT CHANG

Wang Wei

In my later years I care for nothing but quietness
All things now
            inconsequent to my heart
I take thought for myself
                No splendid plans
I only know
            I'll go back to my house in the woods
Pine wind blowing
                loosening my sash
Mountain moon
            on my hands playing the lute
You ask
        if I've construed the poles of being
Listen! a fisherman's song
                    going far up the river.

(translated by C. H. Kwock and Vincent McHugh)

LEAVE-TAKING NEAR SHOKU

Li Po (699–762)
"Sanso, King of Shoku, built roads"

They say the roads of Sanso are steep,
Sheer as the mountains.
The walls rise in a man's face,
Clouds grow out of the hill
    at his horse's bridle.
Sweet trees are on the paved way of the Shin,
Their trunks burst through the paving,
And freshets are bursting their ice
    in the midst of Shoku, a proud city.

Men's fates are already set,
There is no need of asking diviners.

(translated by Ezra Pound)

ANCIENT WISDOM, RATHER COSMIC

Li Po

So-Shu dreamed,
And having dreamed that he was a bird, a bee,
      and a butterfly,
He was uncertain why he should try to feel like
      anything else,
Hence his contentment.

(translated by Ezra Pound)

POEM

Liu Chang-ch'ing (fl. 733)

There go the wild
crane: retreating
with a lone cloud.

How can wild
crane live
where mankind is?

Listen to me:
don't buy on
Yao-chou hills—

today's men
already
know the place.

*(translated by Lenore Mayhew and
William McNaughton)*

6 4

A GOOD PLACE TO LIVE

Tu Fu (712–770)

The "Wet-Flower
    Stream" 's waters
        water the western bank.
For me,
    they chose
        a wooded dam's retreat.
I knew, once
    out of the city,
        the 'world's business' would fade
And there would be
    clear waters
        to melt the traveler's grief.
Beyond counting,
    dragonflies
        in twos leap and dip;
A single pair
    of Mandarin Ducks
        facing, dive and drift.
Let's go east
    ten thousand li!
        I'm borne on a moment's urge
Start out
    to the North Slope
        and set afloat the skiff.

POEM

Wei Ying-wu (773–828)

I wanted to see you
this autumn night

Walked around,
sang under
the cold stars.

In the empty hills,
a pine cone fell—

Were you still
awake?
but hiding out?

*(translated by Lenore Mayhew and
William McNaughton)*

POEM

Chia Tao (788–843)

I stopped to ask a young boy
      just below the pines.
He said, "My master must have gone
      to pick wild vines."
But deeply settled clouds
      lie on the mountain's face,
And when he looks for herbs
      he might be anyplace.

(translated by Lenore Mayhew)

SOUTH OF THE LAKE, EARLY IN JANUARY, I GREET LI YING, M.A.

Tu Mu (803–852)

I seek delight
   seizing the time
      time that has gotten late.
I face the wine
   matching songs
      songs that won't take shape.
Ten thousand li
   in the evening hills:
      kingfishers, flock upon swarm;
A single stream—
   the cold water
      is clear, shallows and deeps.
A man of genius
   takes his wine
      to wash away events.
Uncertain life—
   save poems,
      utterly oppressive a name.
I look at blossoming
   white duckweed.
      The shoot is ready to spill.
In snow to boat,
   greet each other,
      were the end of idle game.[12]

I LIKE THIS ROOM

Tuan Ch'eng-shih (fl. 842)

I like this room.
My heart's unmoved by the world's drift.
I sit facing the tree outside:
West: north: east the shadow shifts.

31

THE MAGIC PILLOW

by Shen Chi-chi (8th Century)

In the seventh year of K'ai Yuan (719 A.D.) a Taoist priest by the name of Lü Weng, who had acquired the magic of the immortals, was traveling on the road to Hantan. He stopped at an inn and was sitting and resting with his back against his bag when he was joined in a very genial conversation by a young man named Lu Sheng, who wore a plain, short coat and rode a black colt and who had stopped at the inn on his way to the fields. After a while Lu Sheng suddenly sighed and said, looking at his shabby clothes, "It is because fate is against me that I have been such a failure in life!" "Why do you say that in the midst of such a pleasant conversation?" Lü Weng said, "For as far as I can see you suffer from nothing and appear to enjoy the best of health." "This is mere existence," Lu Sheng said. "I do not call this life." "What then do you call life?" asked the priest, whereupon the young man answered, "A man ought to achieve great things and make a name for himself; he should be a general at the head of an expedition or a great minister at court, preside over sumptuous banquets and order the orchestra to play what he likes, and cause his clan to prosper and his own family to wax rich—these things make what I call life. I have devoted myself to study and have enriched myself with travel; I used to think that rank and title were mine for the picking, but now at the prime of life I still have to labor in the fields. What do you call this if not failure?"

After he finished speaking he felt a sudden drowsiness. The innkeeper was steaming some millet at the time. Lü Weng reached into his bag and took out a pillow and gave it to Lu Sheng, saying, "Rest your head on this pillow; it will enable you to fulfill your wishes." The pillow was made of green porcelain and had an opening at each end. Lu Sheng bent his head toward it and as he did so the opening grew large and bright, so that he was able to crawl into it. He found himself back home. A few months later he married the daughter of the Tsui Family of Chingho, who was very beautiful and made him exceedingly happy. His wealth increased and the number of luxuries with which he surrounded himself multiplied day by day. The following year he passed the examinations and thus "discarded his hempen coat" and joined the ranks at court. He was made a member of the imperial secretariat and had the honor of composing occasional poems at the emperor's command. After serving a term as inspector of Weinan, he was promoted to the Censorate, and made secretary in attendance. In the latter capacity he took part in the drafting of important decrees.

There followed a succession of provincial posts, in one of which, as the governor of Shensi, he built a canal eighty li in length, which brought so many benefits to the people of the region that they commemorated his achievement upon stone. Next he was made governor of the metropolitan district. In the same year the Emperor's campaigns against the encroaching barbarians reached a critical stage, and when the Turfan and Chulung hordes invested Kuachou and Shachou and menaced the region of the Ho and the Huang, the Emperor, in his search for new talent, made Lu Sheng associate director of the Censorate and governor-general of the Hosi Circuit. Lu Sheng routed the barbarians, killing seven thousand men. He conquered nine hundred li of territory and built three cities to guard the frontier. The people of the frontier region built a monument on the Chuyen Mountain to commemorate his exploits, and when he returned to court he was received with triumphal honors and was made vice-president of the Board of Civil Service and then president of the Board of Revenue. No name carried so much prestige as his and he had the universal acclaim of popular sentiment, but these incurred the jealousy of the other ministers at court, and as a result of their slanderous attacks he was banished to a provincial post. Three years later, however, he was recalled to court and for more than ten years, with Hsiao Sung and P'ei Kuangt'ing, he held the reins of government. Sometimes he received as many as three confidential messages from the Emperor in one day and was ever ready to assist His Majesty with his wise counsel.

Then again he fell victim to the jealousy of his colleagues. They charged him with conspiring with frontier generals to overthrow the dynasty and caused him to be thrown into prison. When the guards came to arrest him, he was stricken with terror and perplexity and said to his wife and sons: "Back in Shantung we have five hundred acres of good land, quite sufficient to keep us from cold and hunger. Why should I have sought rank and title, which in the end have only brought calamity? It is now too late to wish that I could again ride back and forth on the Hantan road as I once did, wearing my plain hempen coat!" Thereupon he drew his sword and attempted to kill himself, but was prevented from doing so by his wife. All those implicated in the plot were executed but Lu Sheng escaped death through the intercession of one of the eunuchs in the confidence of the Emperor. His sentence was commuted to exile to Huanchou. In a few years the Emperor, having ascertained his innocence, recalled him, made him president of the Imperial Council, and gave him the title of Duke of Yenkuo.

He had five sons, all of whom were gifted and were admitted into official ranks. They all married daughters of influential families of the time and presented him with more than ten grandchildren. And so he lived for over fifty years, during which he was twice banished to the frontier wilds only to be re-called to court, vindicated, and given greater honors than before. He was given to extravagance and was addicted to pleasures. His inner apartments were filled with dancers and beautiful women, and in-numerable were the gifts of fertile lands, mansions, fleet horses, and such treasures that the Emperor be-stowed upon him.

When advanced age made him wish to retire from court life, his petitions were repeatedly refused. When at last he fell ill, emissaries sent by the Em-peror to inquire after his condition followed upon one another's heels and there was nothing left undone that eminent physicians could do. But all was in vain and one night he died, whereupon he woke up with a start and found himself lying as before in the road-side inn, with Lü Weng sitting by his side and the millet that his host was cooking still not yet done. Everything was as it had been before he dozed off. "Could it be that I have been dreaming all this while?" he said, rising to his feet. "Life as you would have it is but like that," said Lü Weng. For a long while the young man reflected in silence, then he said, "I now know at least the way of honor and dis-grace and the meaning of poverty and fortune, the reciprocity of gain and loss and the mystery of life and death, and I owe all this knowledge to you. Since you have thus deigned to instruct me in the vanity of ambition, dare I refuse to profit thereby?" With this he bowed profoundly to Lü Weng and went away.

(translated by Wang Chi-chen)

32

THE JAPANESE

One color goes, goes
before it's seen—a flower's color,
    and this flower is
the flower in a man's heart,
the heart of a man in the world.

—Ono no Komachi (fl. 850)

(translated by Lenore Mayhew)

Beside the highway,
the hollyhock-flower is
eaten by my horse.

—Bashõ (1644–1694)

After it got dark
I began to want to change
the way I graft' it.

—Issa (1656–1723)

Walked all day in snow—
as the city comes in sight,
they're closing the gates.

—Buson (1715–1783)

All day, plowing the field—
the cloud that never moved
is gone.

—Buson

33

THE MODERNS

ROAD

Yamamura Bochō (1885–1925)

There's no road in front of you
that's the print of your own foot
here? O, here is the world's road
here? here is everyone's road.
I speak of
the road the dragonfly cuts.

FINE WORK WITH PITCH AND COPPER
William Carlos Williams (1883–1963)

Now they are resting
in the fleckless light
separately in unison

like the sacks
of sifted stone stacked
regularly by twos

about the flat roof
ready after lunch
to be opened and strewn

The copper in eight
foot strips has been
beaten lengthwise

down the center at right
angles and lies ready
to edge the coping

One still chewing
picks up a copper strip
and runs his eye along it

CLASSIC SCENE

William Carlos Williams

A power-house
in the shape of
a red brick chair
90 feet high

on the seat of which
sit the figures
of two metal
stacks—aluminum—

commanding an area
of squalid shacks
side by side—
from one of which

buff smoke
streams while under
a grey sky
the other remains

passive today—

PITY THIS BUSY MONSTER, MANUNKIND

E. E. Cummings (1894–1962)

pity this busy monster,manunkind,

not. Progress is a comfortable disease;
your victim (death and life safely beyond)

plays with the bigness of his littleness
—electrons deify one razorblade
into a mountainrange;lenses extend

unwish through curving wherewhen till unwish
returns on its unself.

        A world of made
is not a world of born—pity poor flesh

and trees, poor stars and stones, but never this
fine specimen of hypermagical

ultraomnipotence. We doctors know

a hopeless case if—listen:there's a hell
of a good universe next door;let's go

n
OthI
n

g can

s
urPas
s

the m

y
SteR
y

of

s
tilLnes
s

—*E. E. Cummings*

seeker of truth
follow no path
all paths lead where
truth is here

—*E. E. Cummings*

8 1

BIRD

Lenore Mayhew (born 1924)

Caught in the lens
                I saw it all:
the insolent whistle
                in the soft throat
the blue-gauze side-feathers
the angled tail
the cockade
the scarlet
and the mad black eye
                of the cardinal.

A NOTE ON THESE TRANSLATIONS

I am told that the *Tao Te Ching* has been translated into English more times by far than any other Chinese book. Since the objectives of this '*Taoist Vision*' lie to some extent through new translations of *Tao Te Ching* passages, I should perhaps try to give some idea of why my translations differ—as they often do—from earlier versions. I hope that by doing this I may get better criticism from my readers who know classical Chinese, for it will be easier now for them to dissociate failures of information from mistakes of method.

Most translators that I have read try to tell you what Lao Tzu means rather than what he says. Lao Tzu didn't get it quite right the first time, so the translator (whether into English, or modern Chinese, or other classical Chinese than the original text) has got to put it into his own new words. I think the reader can see better what Lao Tzu means from a translation that says what Lao Tzu says than from a translation that says what Lao Tzu means, and that is the assumption on the basis of which I have made these translations.

At about the same time as Professor Tung T'ung-ho was writing his piece—you'd have to call it a "pioneering" work—his piece "Etymological Study as A Key to the Interpretation of the Chinese Classics—A Suggestion,"[13] I was working on the poetic uses of etymology in *Shih Ching*.[14] Although the poets may use polyptoton and paregmenon slightly differently than the writers of prose, there certainly (I say) is no prose text in Chinese to the study of which rhetorical theory more profitably may be turned than the *Tao Te Ching*. I have used it, and especially have used the etymological relationship of words, both in deciding what the original text said, and in deciding how best to say the same thing in English.

I have found most useful in studying etymological factors Bernhard Karlgren's "Cognate Words in the Chinese Phonetic Series,"[15] and *Word Families in Chinese* (Stockholm, 1934). Karlgren's work, of course, rests very firmly on the basis of native Chinese scholarship. Such work as *Shuo-wen t'ung-hsun ting-shen,* by Chu Chun-sheng (1788–1858), can be used as an etymological dictionary even if, as Professor Tung observes, "from the viewpoint of contemporary linguistics, it has a fault or two." I also have found invaluable Janusz Chmielewski's work in *Rocznik Orientalistyczny.*

NOTES

1. E. E. Cummings, *Eimi*.

2. Ssu-ma Ch'ien set up for all time the main form of Chinese biography, and even in modern encyclopedias you find that biographical information is given in the same way, in the same order. For a parody of the biographical form, see below, Chap. 28.

3. The reader should know that where earlier translators deal with *"wu-wei"* as if it meant 'non-action,' I have translated and treated it as 'anti-action.' If Lao Tzu had meant "non-action," he never would have said "the longest journey begins under your very foot." He would have said "under the seat of your pants." *Wu-wei* as sloth? catatonia? Putting it mildly, that's to misunderstand the *Tao Te Ching*.

    Everybody should make up his own mind whether *wu-wei,* and the rest of it, is relevant, or whether Lao Tzu was just playing with words. After I lectured at Oberlin once on Taoism, a Conservatory student—she was a piano major—told me that her instructors taught her, "If you want successfully to play a passage *legato,* you must detach the notes."

Another time, a young oboist who had studied with "the world's greatest oboist," told me that his maestro said, "The notes mean nothing. All the music is between the notes."

Frank Lloyd Wright, as you may know, was delighted to find in Lao Tzu the statement, "You cut material into doors and windows to make a room, and its usefulness as a room is just where it isn't. So you take what of it there is, to use what of it there isn't." Not that Wright learned anything about building from the statement, but it confirmed a principle which Wright himself had discovered and according to which he had built for years. I write this as I sit in the Old Imperial Hotel in Tokyo, and I defy anyone who has been here, or in other Wright buildings in which the principle is used, to deny that it gives the building a different feel, or "soul," and that this different feeling has to do with the "where it isn't."

Paul Arnold asks his drawing students to look at an old kitchen chair which he has placed in front of the room. He asks them to draw the spaces between the slats on the back of the chair. The students cannot do it; they all draw the back of the chair instead. Westerners find it hard to see with a Taoist eye.

The Chinese science of war can be traced to one book—Sun Tzu's *Art of War* (sixth century B.C.). Even a casual reading will soon show how much *Art of War* exploits the "anti-action" principle. One or two Western scholars recently have shown that "guerrilla war" comes right out of Sun Tzu's book. The "one principle" which informs it is still anti-action.

Saul Alinsky uses the principle in civil-rights agitation. He says, "When we begin to work, we make up a list of our weaknesses. Then we decide which of them is the weakest, and we try to turn it to our advantage." I don't know whether he thinks of this as Taoist or not. He calls it "social jiu-jitsu," and jiu-jitsu is another Oriental discipline developed on the principle of anti-action.

4. If this sounds like foolishness, think about the year Mao Tse-tung spent with his friend, dressed up in old clothes, knocking around China learning "to talk like a peasant."

5. In Chapters 12, 13, and 14, we find Lao Tzu discussing subjects which, for the Confucians, lie at the basis of social order. Mencius says, "The 'four foundations' are humanitas, equity, ritual, and education. If these four foundations can be established throughout the society, they will be sufficient to create and preserve world order" (II, i, vi, 5–7).

6. The passage also could be translated: "Therefore, lose the Tao, and next, effect; lose the effect, and next, humanitas; lose humanitas, and next, equity; lose equity, and next *li* [ritual and manners]." It depends partly on whether you want your translation to sound like a lecture or like a conversation. The equations are: 1) *te,* energy/effect; 2) *Jen,* good nature/humanitas; 3) *i,* sense of proportion/equity. I prefer "good nature" and "sense of proportion" for this chapter, although I go back to "humanitas" and "equity" for the next chapter.

7. This passage really upsets most "men of good will." I believe that it would be very easy to "water down"

Lao Tzu's meaning and so destroy the passage. But I will say that by my lights, Lao Tzu is talking in part about *terminology*, and I have tried to indicate it by the use of single quotes in my translation. Cf. Hemingway, "There were many words that you could not stand to hear and finally only the names of places had dignity. Certain numbers were the same way and certain dates . . ." (*A Farewell to Arms,* Chapter 27).

8. "The six relationships"—one way of classifying the social relations of paramount importance in which each man finds himself: to his father, to his mother, to his elder brothers, to his younger brothers, to his wife, and to his children.

9. If you think this is far-fetched, consider the elation of my friend O. He is in labor-management relations, and I still remember the ecstasy on his face when he reported to me, in 1954, on a psychologists' monograph he had just read. "They discovered," said O., "that if the workers in a factory have been restless and complaining, and you change conditions some, no matter how—you even can change them for the worse—the workers will shut up for awhile." Lest I be suspected of class bias, let me hasten to say that I do not think the "three nuts in the morning" principle can be applied effectively only in factories.

10. *Cf.* the story in Mencius II, i, ii: "There was a man of Sung, who got anxious because the corn was growing so slow. So he went into the field and pulled on the corn to help it grow and then, exhausted, he went home. At home, he said to his family, "Am I tired! Today I have been helping the corn to grow." And his son ran out to the field and looked and came

back shouting, "Pa! Pa! The corn is all withered and dead!" Mencius continues, "There are few in the world who do not help the corn to grow, few who see that it does no good and so let the grain alone."

11. Made up of Pound's regular and *aliter* versions, so as more nearly to match the form and sequence of lines in the Chinese.

12. The last line alludes to the following story—a very good Taoist story. A man lived south of China's biggest lake. One evening, when the snow was falling, he decided to visit his friend who lived north of the lake. So he bundled up and went down to the docks, but none of the regular boats was running, and he could not persuade any of the boatmen to take him across, because of the weather. Finally, offering an exorbitant fare, he talked an old fisherman into taking him to the other side of the lake. They untied and set out on the water. After some time, about as they reached the middle of the lake, the man said to the fisherman, "Turn around! I want to go back."

The fisherman was very angry. He said, "Get me out on a night like this! Talk me into taking you across the lake to see your friend! Now that we are half way there, you say 'Turn around and go back!' What's the matter with you? Are you crazy?"

The man replied, "Earlier tonight, when I made my deal with you, what I wanted to do was visit my friend. So I followed my desire and set out. Now what I want to do is go home, and so I shall follow my desire and go home. What is wrong with that?"

The fisherman turned his boat and took the man home.

13. The article was published posthumously in *Bulletin of the Institute of History and Philology of Academia Sinica* XXXVI, i (1965), pp. 1–9.

14. See my *Shih Ching Rhetoric: Schemes of Words* (Ann Arbor: University Microfilms, 1965), pp. 136–175. See also Chaps. 14 and 15, my *The Book of Songs*. (New York: Twayne, to be published.)

15. Published in *Bulletin of the Museum of Far Eastern Antiquities* XXVII (1956).

9 0

Selected Ann Arbor Paperbacks
Works of enduring merit

For a complete list of Ann Arbor Paperback titles write:
THE UNIVERSITY OF MICHIGAN PRESS ANN ARBOR